DARK PSYCHOLOGY

This document is geared towards providing exact and reliable information in regards to the topic and issue covered. The publication is sold with the idea that the publisher is not required to render accounting, officially permitted, or otherwise, qualified services. If advice is necessary, legal or professional, a practiced individual in the profession should be ordered.

Table of Contents

10. Targets the victim

11. Positive reinforcement

12. Moves the goal posts

13. Diversion

14. Sarcasm

15. Guilt tripping

16. Flattery

17. Playing the innocent card

18. Over the top aggression

19. Isolation

20. Feigns love and empathy

TYPES OF MANIPULATORS

The chronic victim

The permanently disappointed

The masked braggart

The inquisitor

The martyr

The sower of ideas

The selective listener

TRAITS OF MANIPULATORS

1. Manipulative People Play the Victim

2. Manipulative People Tell Distorted or Half Truths

3. Manipulative People Are Passive-Aggressive

4. Manipulative People Will Pressure You

5. Manipulative People Will Guilt Trip You

6. Manipulative People Give The Silent Treatment

7. Manipulative People Don't Work To Resolve Problems

8. Manipulative People Prefer To Play On Their Homeground

9. Manipulative People Rationalize Their Behavior

10. Manipulative People Shake Your Confidence

SIGNS OF MANIPULATION

1. Charm and Niceness

2. Denial

3. Lying

4. Generous With Favors and Gifts

5. Excessive Compliments and Flattery

6. Forced Teaming

7. Good First Impression

8. Pretending to Be a Victim

9. Silent Treatment

10. Appearing to Be Selfless

11. Guilt Tripping

12. Shaming

13. Intimidation

14. Gas Lighting

15. Rationalization

16. Diversion

17. Unsettling Stare

INTRODUCTION

Dark Psychology is the study of the human condition as it relates to the psychological nature of people to prey upon other people motivated by criminal and/or deviant drives that lack purpose and general assumptions of instinctual drives and social sciences theory. All of humanity has the potentiality to victimize humans and other living creatures. While many restrain or sublimate this tendency, some act upon these impulses. Dark Psychology seeks to understand those thoughts, feelings, perceptions and subjective processing systems that lead to predatory behavior that is antithetical to contemporary understandings of human behavior.

Dark Psychology assumes that criminal, deviant and abusive behaviors are purposive and have some rational, goal-oriented motivation 99% of the time. It is the remaining 1%, Dark Psychology parts from Adlerian theory and Teleology. Dark

Psychology encompasses all that makes us who we are in relationship to our dark side. All cultures, faiths and humanity have this proverbial cancer. From the moment we are born to the time of death, there is a side hidden within us that some have called "Evil" and others have defined as criminal, deviant or psychopathic.

Understanding dark psychology is not only a defensive measure. There are ideas and principles contained within the world of dark psychology that can help you get ahead in your personal and professional endeavors. No one is asking you to become a psychopath, but surely you could use a little more power in your day-to-day life.

Dark Psychology posits there are people who commit these same acts and do so not for power, money, sex, retribution or any other known purpose. They commit horrid acts without a goal. Simplified, their ends do not justify their means. There are people who violate and injure others for the sake of doing so. Within in all of us is this potential. A potential to harm others without cause, explanation, or purpose is the area explored. Dark Psychology assumes this dark potential is incredibly complex and even more difficult to define.

WHAT IS DARK PSYCHOLOGY?

Dark Psychology is the art and science of manipulation and mind control. While Psychology is the study of human behavior and is central to our thoughts, actions, and interactions, the term Dark Psychology is the phenomenon by which people use tactics of motivation, persuasion, manipulation, and coercion to get what they want.

Psychology, the understanding of the human mind and the way it works, is a topic central to the existence of mankind. Psychology underpins everything from advertising to finance, crime to religion, and love to hate. Someone who understands psychological principles holds the key to human influence, a key few other people possess.

Obtaining psychological knowledge is often a difficult task. Like all of mankind's most advanced secrets, psychological knowledge is buried deep within the pages of dense journals and kept out of the reach of the general public. To distill this powerful information into a useful form would require someone to delve through countless books and journals, attempting to separate the useful from the useless.

Dark psychology is at work in the world. You might not like this fact, but you can't change it. So you have a choice: either try to remain ignorant of something powerful and risk becoming its next victim, or take control of your situation and learn to protect yourself, and those you love, from people who would ruin you through their ruthless psychological exploitation.

Dark Psychology encompasses all that makes us who we are in relationship to our dark side. All cultures, all faiths and all humanity have this proverbial cancer. From the moment we are born to the time of death, there is a side lurking within us all that some have called evil and others have defined as criminal, deviant, and pathological. Dark Psychology introduces a third philosophical construct that views these behaviors different from religious dogmas and contemporary social science theories.

"It is the individual who is not interested in his fellow men who has the greatest difficulties in life and provides the greatest injury to others. It is from among such individuals that all human failures spring. "Alfred Adler

Dark Psychology posits there are people who commit these same acts and do so not for power, money, sex, retribution or any other known purpose. They commit these horrid acts without a goal. Simplified, their ends do not justify their means. There are people who violate and injure others for the sake of doing so. Within in all of us is this potential. A potential to harm others without cause, explanation, or purpose is the area this writer explores. Dark Psychology assumes this dark potential is incredibly complex and even more difficult to define.

Dark Psychology assumes we all have the potential for predator behaviors and this potential has access to our thoughts, feelings and perceptions. As you will read throughout this manuscript, we all have this potential, but only a few of us acts upon them. All of us have had thoughts and feelings, at one time or another, of wanting to behave in a brutal manner. We all have had thoughts of wanting to hurt others severely without mercy. If you are honest with yourself, you will have to agree you have had thoughts and feeling of wanting to commit heinous acts.

Given the fact, we consider ourselves a benevolent species; one would like to believe we think these thoughts and feelings would be non-existent. Unfortunately, we all have these thoughts, and luckily, never act upon them. Dark Psychology poses there are people who have these same thoughts, feelings, and perceptions, but act upon them in either premeditated or impulsive ways. The obvious difference is they act upon them while others simply have fleeting thoughts and feelings of doing so.

Dark Psychology posits that this predator style is purposive and has some rational, goal-oriented motivation. Religion, philosophy, psychology, and other dogmas have attempted cogently to define Dark Psychology. It is true most human behavior, related to evil actions, is purposive and goal oriented, but Dark Psychology assumes there is an area where purposive behavior and goal oriented motivation seems to become nebulous. There is a continuum of Dark Psychology victimization ranging from thoughts to pure psychopathic deviance without any apparent rationality or purpose. This continuum, Dark Continuum, helps to conceptualize the philosophy of Dark Psychology.

Dark Psychology addresses that part of the human psyche or universal human condition that allows for and may even impel predatory behavior. Some characteristics of this behavioral tendency are, in many cases, its lack of obvious rational motivation, its universality and its lack of predictability. Dark Psychology assumes this universal human condition is different or an extension of evolution. Let us look at some very basic tenets of evolution. First, consider we evolved from other animals and we presently are the paragon of all animal life. Our frontal lobe has allowed us to become the apex creature. Now let us assume that being apex creatures does not make us completely removed from our animal instincts and predatory nature.

"The greater the feeling of inferiority that has been experienced, the more powerful is the urge to conquest and the more violent the emotional agitation."

Assuming this is true if you subscribe to evolution, then you believe that all behavior relates to three primary instincts. Sex, aggression, and the instinctual drive to self-sustain are the three primary human drives. Evolution follows the tenets of survival of the fittest and replication of the species. We and all other life forms behave in a manner to procreate and survive. Aggression occurs for the purposes of marking our territory, protecting our territory and ultimately winning the right to procreate. It sounds rational, but it is no longer part of the human condition in the purest sense.

Our power of thought and perception has made us both the apex of species and the apex of practicing brutality. If you have ever watched a nature documentary, this writer is sure you cringe and feel sorrow for the antelope ripped to shreds by a pride of lions. Although brutal and unfortunate, the purpose for the violence fits the evolutionary model of self- preservation. The lions kill for food, which is required for survival. Male animals fight to the death, at times, for the rite of territory or the will to power. All these acts, violent and brutal, evolution explains.

When animals hunt, they often stalk and kill the youngest, weakest, or females of the group. Although this reality sounds psychopathic, the reason for their chosen prey is to reduce their own probability for injury or death. All animal life acts and behaves in this manner. All their brutal, violent and bloody actions relate to the theory of evolution, natural selection and instinct for survival and reproduction. As you will learn after reading this manuscript, there are no Dark Psychology applications when it comes to the rest of life on our planet. We, humans are the ones to possess what Dark Psychology attempts to explore.

Theories of evolution, natural selection and animal instincts, and their theoretical tenets, seem to dissolve when we look at the human condition. We are the only creatures on the face of the earth that preys on each other without the reason of procreation for the survival of the species. Humans are the only creatures that prey upon others for inexplicable motivations. Dark Psychology addresses that part of the human psyche or universal human condition that allows for and may even impel predatory behavior. Dark

Psychology assumes there is something intrapsychic that influences our actions and is anti-evolutionary. We are the only species that will murder one another for reasons other than survival, food, territory or procreation.

Philosophers and ecclesiastical writers over the centuries have attempted to explain this phenomenon. We will delve into some of these historical interpretations of malicious human behavior. Only we humans can harm others with a complete lack of obvious rational motivation. Dark Psychology assumes there is a part of us, because we are human, which fuels dark and vicious behaviors.

As you will read, this place or realm within all of our beings is universal. There is no group of people walking the face of the earth now, before, or in the future who do not possess this dark side. Dark Psychology believes this facet of the human condition lacks reason and logical rationality. It is part of all of us and there is no known explanation.

Dark Psychology assumes this dark side is also unpredictable. Unpredictable in the understanding of who acts upon these dangerous impulses, and even more unpredictable of the lengths some will go with their sense of mercy completely negated. There are people who rape, murder, torture, and violate without cause or purpose. Dark Psychology speaks to these actions of acting as a predator seeking out human prey without clearly defined purposes. As humans, we are incredibly dangerous to ourselves and every other living creature. The reasons are many and Dark Psychology attempts to explore those dangerous elements.

THE DARK TRIAD

The 'dark triad' refers to the personality traits narcissism, Machiavellianism and psychopathy.

1. Narcissism

First of all is Narcissism. This term came about because of the Greek myth of Narcissus, a young man who fell in love with his reflection after looking at himself in a pond of water. He became so engrossed in it that he fell into the water and drowned.

Consequently, narcissism has become synonymous with unhealthy self-love. Narcissists are prideful, lack empathy for others and have a low tolerance for criticism. Narcissists have no qualms about manipulating others for their gain. They also put others down. What is noteworthy is that people are narcissistic to different degrees.

2. Machiavellianism

16th-century Italian diplomat, Niccolo Machiavelli gets the credit for the term 'Machiavellianism.' It came about because critics felt that his book 'The Prince,' condoned cunning, deceit, and self-interest. The book said that these qualities were necessary for political gain.

Therefore, people with such traits take lying to new heights. They have no morals or feelings for others.

3. Psychopathy

Those with psychopathic traits have no feelings for others. Because they have no remorse, they show anti-social behaviors. Many of them are explosive and controlling.
Note that having these qualities does not make a person a psychopath. Psychopaths are criminals. Though those with psychopathic qualities are unpredictable, they are not necessarily criminals.

A study shows that Dark Triad traits are not hereditary but due to environmental factors.
Those who have the Dark Triad tend to show behaviors that blend the worst of the three worlds. They have many relationships, often behind their partners' backs. They are also aggressive.

How Would You Know That Someone Has the Dark Triad?

The first step to coping with someone who has the Dark Triad is to recognize its signs. Because they are complex, psychologists are still trying to understand them.
They used to measure each quality separately, but there is now an easier way to spot them.

The Dirty Dozen Scale, shows if a person has the Dark Triad.

I manipulate others.
I lie to others.
I flatter others.
I use others for my gain.
I lack remorse.
I am not concerned about the morality of my actions.
I am mean and insensitive.
I am a cynical person.
I need the admiration of others.
I crave attention.
I want favors from others.
I seek status and prestige.

After answering the questions, psychologists would rate a person with a score of 12 to 84. Therefore, the higher the score, the greater the possibility of having the Dark Triad.

How to Deal with People with Dark Triad Traits

How would you escape the clutches of a person with the Dark Triad? There is no easy way to go about it. However, there are steps you can take to reduce their negativity.

First of all, people with these qualities have difficulty managing their anger. Those with psychopathic traits, for example, are bad-tempered. At work, their anger may show in passive-aggressive behaviors like ignoring people or sulking. It is important not to take the behavior personally because it is often not about you.

Also, take some time to listen to their concerns and counsel them about their behavior. Stand your ground. If they are bullies, confront them and hold them responsible.

Another way you can cope with such characters is to avoid contact whenever possible. Use emails if you need to get in touch with them. People with the Dark Triad are often charming. Experts suggest that they rely on their looks to get their way.

The Dark Triad, in conclusion, can ruin relationships. You can cope with it if you recognize it. Being assertive and savvy also helps.

DARK PSYCHOLOGY AND MANIPULATION

Dark Psychology is the art and science of manipulation and mind control. While Psychology is the study of human behavior and is central to our thoughts, actions, and interactions, the term Dark Psychology is the phenomenon by which people use tactics of motivation, persuasion, manipulation, and coercion to get what they want.

Dark Psychology Triad

Narcissism – Egotism, grandiosity, and lack of empathy.

Machiavellianism – Uses manipulation to deceive and exploit people and has no sense of morality.

Psychopathy – Often charming and friendly yet is characterized by impulsivity, selfishness, lack of empathy, and remorselessness.

None of us want to be a victim of manipulation, but it happens quite often. We may not be subject to someone specifically in the Dark Triad, but normal, everyday people like you and I face dark psychology tactics on a daily basis.

These tactics are often found in commercials, internet ads, sales techniques, and even our manager's behaviors. If you have kids (especially teenagers) you will most definitely experience these tactics as your children experiment with behaviors to get what they want and seek autonomy. In fact, covert manipulation and dark persuasion are often used by people you trust and love. Here are some of the tactics used most often by normal, everyday people.

Love Flooding – Compliments, affection or buttering someone up to make a request

Lying – Exaggeration, untruths, partial truths, untrue stories

Love Denial – Withhold attention and affection

Withdrawal – Avoiding the person or silent treatment

Choice restriction – Giving certain choice options that distract from the choice you don't want someone to make

Reverse Psychology – Tell a person one thing or to do something with an intention to motivate them to do the opposite which is really what you desire.

Semantic Manipulation – Using words that are assumed to have a common or mutual definition, yet the manipulator later tells you he or she has a different definition and understanding of the conversation. Words are powerful and import.

While some people who use theses dark tactics know exactly what they are doing and they are intentional about manipulating you to getting what they want, others use dark and unethical tactics without being fully aware of it. Many of these people learned the tactics during childhood from their parents. Others learned the tactics in their teenage years or adulthood by happenstance. They used a manipulation tactic unintentionally and it worked. They got what they wanted. Therefore, they continue to use tactics that help them get their way.

In some cases, people are trained to use these tactics. Training programs that teach dark, unethical psychological and persuasion tactics are typically sales or marketing programs. Many of these programs use dark tactics to create a brand or sell a product with the sole purpose of serving themselves or their company, not the customer. Many of these training programs convince people that using such tactics are okay and is for the benefit of the buyer. Because, of course, their lives will be much better when they purchase the product or service.

Who uses Dark Psychology and manipulation tactics? Here's a list of people who seem to use these tactics the most.

Narcissists – People who are truly narcissistic (meeting clinical diagnosis) have an inflated sense of self-worth. They need others to validate their belief of being superior. They have dreams of being worshipped and adored. They use dark psychology tactics, manipulation, and unethical persuasion to maintain.

Sociopaths – People who are truly sociopathic (meeting clinical diagnosis), are often charming, intelligent, yet impulsive. Due to a lack of emotionality and ability to feel remorse they use dark tactics to build a superficial relationship and then take advantage of people.

Attorneys – Some attorneys focus so intently on winning their case that they resort to using dark persuasion tactics to get the outcome they want.

Politicians – Some politicians use dark psychological tactics and dark persuasion tactics to convince people they are right and to get votes.

Sales People – Many salespeople become so focused on achieving a sale that they use dark tactics to motivate and persuade someone to buy their product.

Leaders – Some leaders use dark tactics to get compliance, greater effort, or higher performance from their subordinates.

Public Speakers – Some speakers use dark tactics to heighten the emotional state of the audience knowing it leads to selling more products at the back of the room.

Selfish People – This can be anyone who has an agenda of self before others. They will use tactics to meet their own needs first, even at someone else's expense. They don't mind win-lose outcomes.

To differentiate between those motivation and persuasion tactics that are dark and those that are ethical, it's important to assess your intent. We must ask ourselves if the tactics that we are using have an intention to help the other person? It is okay for the intention to be to help you as well, but if it's solely for your benefit, you can easily fall into dark and unethical practices.

Having a mutually beneficial or a "win-win" outcome should be the goal. However, you must be honest with yourself and your belief that the other person will truly benefit. An example of this is a salesperson who believes everyone will benefit from his product and life will be much better for the customer because of the purchase. A salesperson with this mentality can easily fall into using dark tactics to move the person to buy and use an "ends justifies the means" mentality. This opens the person up to any and all tactics to get the sale.

We can ask ourselves the following questions to assess our intention along with our motivation and persuasion tactics:

What is my goal for this interaction? Who benefits and how?

Do I feel good about how I am approaching the interaction?

Am I being totally open and honest?

Will the result of this interaction lead to a long-term benefit for the other person?

Will the tactics I use lead to a more trusting relationship with the other person?

Do you want to be truly successful in your leadership, relationships, parenting, work, and other areas of life? Then assess yourself to determine your current tactics for motivation and persuasion. Doing it right leads to long-term credibility and influence. Doing it wrong (going dark) leads to poor character, broken relationships, and long-term failure because people eventually see through the darkness and realize your intent.

MANIPULATION

WHAT IS MANIPULATION?

Most people engage in periodic manipulation. For example, telling an acquaintance you feel "fine" when you are actually depressed is, technically, a form of manipulation because it controls your acquaintance's perceptions of and reactions to you.

Manipulation can also have more insidious consequences, however, and it is often associated with emotional abuse, particularly in intimate relationships. Most people view manipulation negatively, especially when it harms the physical, emotional, or mental health of the person being manipulated.

While people who manipulate others often do so because they feel the need to control their environment and surroundings, an urge that often stems from deep-seated fear or anxiety, it is not a healthy behavior. Engaging in manipulation may prevent the manipulator from connecting with their authentic self, and being manipulated can cause an individual to experience a wide range of ill effects.

If unaddressed, manipulation can lead to poor mental health outcomes for those who are manipulated. Chronic manipulation in close relationships may also be a sign emotional abuse is taking place, which in some cases, can have a similar effect to trauma—particularly when the victim of manipulation is made to feel guilty or ashamed.

Victims of chronic manipulation may:

Feel depressed
Develop anxiety

Develop unhealthy coping patterns

Constantly try to please the manipulative person

Lie about their feelings

Put another person's needs before their own

Find it difficult to trust others

In some cases, manipulation can be so pervasive that it causes a victim to question their perception of reality. The classic movie Gaslight illustrated one such story, in which a woman's husband subtly manipulated her until she no longer trusted her own perceptions. For example, the husband covertly turned down the gaslights and convinced his wife the dimming light was all in her head.

While most people engage in manipulation from time to time, a chronic pattern of manipulation can indicate an underlying mental health concern.

Manipulation is particularly common with personality disorder diagnoses such as borderline personality (BPD) and narcissistic personality (NPD). For many with BPD, manipulation may be a means of meeting their emotional needs or obtaining validation, and it often occurs when the person with BPD feels insecure or abandoned. As many people with

BPD have witnessed or experienced abuse, manipulation may have developed as a coping mechanism to get needs met indirectly.

Individuals with narcissistic personality (NPD) may have different reasons for engaging in manipulative behavior. As those with NPD may have difficulty forming close relationships, they may resort to manipulation in order to "keep" their partner in the relationship. Characteristics of narcissistic manipulation may include shaming, blaming, playing the "victim," control issues, and gaslighting.

Munchausen syndrome by proxy, during which a caregiver makes another person ill to gain attention or affection, is another condition that is characterized by manipulative behaviors.

EXAMPLES OF MANIPULATIVE BEHAVIOR

Sometimes, people may manipulate others unconsciously, without being fully aware of what they're doing, while others may actively work on strengthening their manipulation tactics. Some signs of manipulation include:

Passive-aggressive behavior
Implicit threats
Dishonesty
Withholding information
Isolating a person from loved ones
Gaslighting
Verbal abuse

Use of sex to achieve goals

As the motives behind manipulation can vary from unconscious to malicious, it's important to identify the circumstances of the manipulation that is taking place. While breaking things off may be critical in situations of abuse, a therapist may help others learn to deal with or confront manipulative behavior from others.

MOST COMMON MANIPULATION TECHNIQUES

1. Lying

Predators are constantly lying about practically everything in their life. They do this to wrong-foot their victim and confuse them. Lying is one of the manipulation techniques psychopaths typically use because they have no qualms about it.

2. Not telling the whole story

This is different to lying as a predator will often keep a key part of the story to themselves in order to put their victim at a disadvantage.

3. Frequent mood swings

Never knowing what mood your partner is going to be in when you get home, whether they'll be happy or angry is a very useful tool to the predator. It keeps their victim off balance and makes them more malleable.

4. Love-bombing and devaluation

Narcissists typically use love bombing as a manipulation tactic, they will go on a charm offensive and get you hooked into thinking this is the best relationship ever, then they'll drop you like a ton of bricks without explanation.

5. Punishment

This can include anything from constant nagging, shouting, the silent treatment, physical violence and mental abuse.

6. Denial

Often the simplest way a predator will manipulate a person is by denying the thing they are accused of ever happening.

7. Spinning the truth

How many times have politicians twisted the facts to suit themselves? This spinning of the truth is often used to disguise bad behaviour by predators such as sociopaths.

8. Minimising

Where a predator will try and play down their actions as not important or damaging and shift the blame onto the victim for overreacting.

9. Plays the victim

The manipulator will themselves take on the role of victim in order to gain sympathy and compassion from those around them. We as humans are naturally drawn to helping people when they are suffering.

10. Targets the victim

When a manipulator accuses the victim of wrongdoing, they are making the victim defend themselves whilst the predator is able to mask their own manipulation techniques. The focus is on the victim, not the accuser.

11. Positive reinforcement

This includes buying expensive presents, praising them, giving money, constantly apologizing for their behaviour, excessive charm and paying lots of attention.

12. Moves the goal posts

You might think you know where you stand with a person, but if they are constantly moving the goal posts in order to confuse you, then it's likely you're dealing with a predator.

13. Diversion

Diverting the conversation away from the perpetrator's act and moving the conversation onto a different topic is a typical way predators manipulate their victims.

14. Sarcasm

A predator will often be sarcastic about their victim in front of others. They do this to lower the self-esteem of the victim and to show others how powerful they are.

15. Guilt tripping

Someone who manipulates will often guilt trip their victim by saying that they don't care about them, or that they are selfish or their life is easy. It all helps to keep that person confused and anxious.

16. Flattery

Using charm, praise or flattering the victim is one way of gaining that person's trust. The victim is naturally happy to receive such compliments but in doing do lowers their guard.

17. Playing the innocent card

A true manipulator will feign utmost shock and confusion at being accused of any wrongdoing. Their surprise is so convincing that the victim may question their own judgement.

18. Over the top aggression

Manipulators often use rage and aggression to shock their victim into submission. The anger is also a tool to shut down any further conversation on the topic as the victim is scared but focused now on controlling the anger, not the original topic.

19. Isolation

It is far easier to keep a person under control if they are isolated from family members and friends who could shed some light and truth on the situation.

20. Feigns love and empathy

Predators such as psychopaths and sociopaths do not know how to love someone other than themselves, and cannot feel empathy, but they can pretend to in order to inveigle others into their lives.

If you watch out for the above manipulation techniques, you can keep yourself out of a predator's clutches.

TYPES OF MANIPULATORS

What people consider to be manipulation might be defined differently case by case. The common outcome is making the target feel seriously uncomfortable if they don't perform the will of the "operator." The different ingredients include guilt, shame or anxiety.

Manipulation has a hidden agenda against straightforward communication. It has to be covert because it serves the manipulator's interest in direct opposition to the target's desires.

Making you feel guilty, ashamed or worried can occur by verbal statements or questions, and it can come in the form of hints, stories, and comparisons. It often happens by the tone of voice, facial expression or gesture.

The chronic victim

This kind of manipulator makes us feel in debt with him. He always tell all the misfortunes he has suffered in life, so we think that for some strange reason we can't even understand, we owe something to him.

Because every time we meet him he has a new disgrace to add to his long list, we do not feel strong enough to become the "monster" that will add a new problem to his life while he is going through a bad time.

The problem is that that person will benefit from that feeling to ask for a favor and make sure that we meet his needs, even at the expense of our own. But if we put ourselves at his feet, he will not hesitate to walk on us to keep telling his misfortunes to others, leaving us with our problems to be solved.

The permanently disappointed

When we love someone, we feel better if we do something that makes him angry rather than disappointed. Disappointment is a difficult weight to bear, we feel very bad when we know we've disappointed someone important to us and we feel bad for doing it.

This type of manipulator knows and plays this card in his favor. Therefore, he will be constantly disappointed. Every time we do something that he do not like or do not meet his needs, that person will not hesitate to make us feel how is disappointed. The problem is that the guilt we feel is so great that we give him reason and we put ourselves to his mercy.

We do not realize that disappointing someone means only that we did not live up to the expectations that this person had for us. Deluding someone means that this person had traced a path for us in our place and we did not follow it. In fact, we have all the right of the world to follow the path we have chosen and we should not feel bad about it.

The masked braggart

The tactic of this manipulator is to make us feel bad or inferior in a veiled way. This person understands that he would not look good if he was always claiming his accomplishments, the others would accuse him immediately of being presumptuous. So he adopts a slimmer strategy: it complains about its achievements, making us feel bad because we are far below his level.

The masked braggart will never tell us directly that we have a few extra pounds, but will complain that he can't wear an "M" size when we wear an "L" or even an "XL". It is the person who complains because he can't run more than 30 kilometers when he knows perfectly that we only run 5 kilometers before we get exhausted

The masked braggart will use his secret technique in all spheres of life, he will compare to us in a subtle way to make us clear that we are not at his height and that we should feel guilty about it. In this way he also presents himself as a kind of idol to be imitated because we put ourselves at its disposal and satisfy his desires.

The inquisitor

This manipulator uses direct criticism as main weapon. His tactic is to make us feel that we are unable to take the reins of our lives, we are not up to the situation and we need to rely on him because everything works.

At first criticisms are subtle and indirect, but with time they will become smoother, they will deepen our self-esteem. In this way he imposes his vision of reality, his rules and values, to the point that we end up seeing ourselves through his eyes.

The Inquisitor is a true master of emotional manipulation and absolutely everything we do or say will be used against us because he will use it to judge us and put us in an uncomfortable position.

In any case, do not let them take control of your life. Do not allow them make you feel guilty or judge you for your decisions based on their judgment.

The martyr

It is one of the worst types of manipulators because justifies his malpractice and selfishness with some higher cause. It could be a religious cause or something more banal, like being a good father or a good mother.

His favorite phrase is "I do it for your good" or "I'm just trying to help you" when we know that's not the case and that the main beneficiary will be him.

However, if we point that out, these people will claim they do not feel like doing it that way, but they do it because it's right. In fact, they can come to tell us that the decision hurt them and cause them to suffer, therefore, they assume the role of martyrs. And the worst thing is that they make us feel horrible because we are not able to appreciate their "sacrifice."

The sower of ideas

These manipulators use a very subtle tactic: they press us with socially accepted and well-seen ideas because we agree with their opinions and decisions.

They usually begin their speech with phrases like "I'm sure you'll agree with..." or "You can't deny that ...". For example, they may say, "You will agree that a good child cares for his mother." These are all generalizations that reflect positive values, but that certainly have many shades and can vary from case to case. But presenting them in this way puts us in a difficult situation where we should answer: "No, I do not agree with what you say."

In fact, this tactic of manipulation consists in presenting these ideas as socially accepted values, so if we do not share them, we automatically turn into bad people, and we will not even have time to argue our view. So they can make us feel bad and manipulate us, unless we find the strength to deny their affirmations.

The selective listener

When we are engaged in a discussion, we can lose patience and say things that we really do not feel or repent of. However, this type of manipulator will cling to that phrase or attitude, and will repeat it until the end of time.

It does not matter what we said before or after. No matter the context we have told it or if we are sorry to apologize, this person will use our mistake to submit us to his will, pointing out how wrong and bad we are.

His strategy is to wait for us to make a mistake, extract it completely from the context and use it to manipulate us emotionally. These persons will focus only on our mistakes, because they are the ones that enable them to achieve their goal, and all the good will simply be erased.

TRAITS OF MANIPULATORS

Manipulative people are the kinds of people who use mental and emotional abuse to one-up you, usually to serve their desires for power or control. Although it can be hard to tell if someone is manipulative when you first meet them, there are several traits that manipulative people often show, which can help tip you off early to this kind of behavior. It's important to look out for manipulation in a relationship, friendship, or with a family member because if you fall prey to a manipulator, it can become difficult to cut yourself loose once you've gotten super involved in their life. Although manipulators are ultimately selfish, they use several schemes and methods to cover this up, which is why it is so hard to identify a manipulative person before it's too late. This list will give you a good understanding of what to look out for in a manipulative person. If you see one or more of these traits in your so-called friends, you better run for the hills. So, without further ado, here are ten bona-fide traits of manipulative people that you should look out for.

1. Manipulative People Play the Victim

Manipulative people are famous for always playing the role of victim and making themselves out to be more innocent than they are. Often, they exaggerate or even make up personal issues so that others feel sorry for them and sympathize with them. In a relationship, this trait of a manipulative person often comes out as dependency or co-dependency. The manipulator may pretend to be weak or frail or in need of constant help to suck the unknowing victim deep into their life. They do this to draw nice people to them like a magnet so that they can later exploit and use them to fulfill their own selfish needs and desires. By playing the victim, the manipulator can seek out and exploit the goodwill, guilty conscience, or protective and nurturing instinct of the target. Have you ever had a friend or family member who constantly asked you to lend them money or asked you to buy things for them, the whole time making you feel guilty for not having done so in the first place? Most likely, you were dealing with a manipulative person, and hopefully, you found your way out of the trap without too much suffering.

2. Manipulative People Tell Distorted or Half Truths

Another horrible personality trait that manipulative people have is lying or distorting the truth so that they always come out right. Great examples of this behavior include excuse making, withholding key information, understatements, exaggeration, or being two-faced. Manipulative people know how to bend the truth to their advantage. They will often omit or hide information that will expose them as being a liar. Manipulators treat all interactions as if they may eventually go to trial and everything they say could be held against them. As a result, they often skirt around the issue or make vague statements so that when confronted, they can claim they "never said that" or that it is "not exactly what they said".

3. Manipulative People Are Passive-Aggressive

An equally annoying personality trait of a manipulative person is that they are more often than not passive-aggressive. A manipulative person may use this sort of behavior to get out of something or to get their way. They may even do this to make you mad without outright doing something insulting towards you. A family member or friend who often forgets something important you have told them or forgets to do something for you that you asked them to may be acting passive-aggressive to manipulate you. It may seem harmless, but it is, in fact, a form of anger, and it is not healthy for their well-being or your sanity.

4. Manipulative People Will Pressure You

Manipulative people, just like salespeople, will often put pressure on another person in hopes of getting you to make a decision before you are really ready to. The manipulator believes that by applying tension and control to you,

you will easily crack and give in to their wishes. Just like those real-estate schemes that pressure you to act fast with the promise of huge profits that don't really exist, manipulative people will do anything to get you to buy into their game or gain some sort of edge over you. So, be wary of anyone who pressures you to give an answer before you are ready, especially if money is involved.

5. Manipulative People Will Guilt Trip You

A manipulative friend or family member will often guilt trip you into doing something that you don't want to do, or vice versa, out of something that you do want to do. The underlying reason for this is their ultimately selfish personality. Guilt trips include unreasonable blaming from the manipulator, along with targeting your soft spot and holding you responsible for their happiness, success, or failures. The manipulator works to target your vulnerabilities and emotional weaknesses so that they can coerce you into doing just what they want you to do. A manipulative person will often make a person whom they are in close relationship with feel guilty if that person is not always available for them. They expect everyone else to help them deal with their problems, but do nothing in return. Anyone who always expects you to be the shoulder that they cry on, but who is never there for you when you need the same, is most likely a manipulative person.

6. Manipulative People Give The Silent Treatment

Have you ever been given the silent treatment from a friend, boyfriend, girlfriend or family member? Chances are you were dealing with a manipulative person. Manipulative people are bullies. One of the ways they bully others is by alienation. Behaviors like ignoring one person in a group, not allowing them to voice their opinions, or leaving them out completely are immature techniques used by manipulative adults to assert their dominance. By exhibiting these behaviors, the manipulative person believes they are coming off as self-confident and powerful. In reality, however, they have low self-esteem and are extremely self-conscious. The only way they know how to make themselves feel better is by hurting others. The next time someone gives you the silent treatment, don't feel bad about writing them off completely. It is a sure sign of a manipulator and should not be taken lightly.

7. Manipulative People Don't Work To Resolve Problems

Manipulators will never take the blame for anything. This also means that they will never contribute to resolving a problem in fear that one day they will be held responsible for their actions. A manipulator's goal is to skate through life without having to step up and take responsibility for anything. When confronted with something by a friend or family member, they will either flat out lie and say they never did anything wrong or will make all sorts of justifications for their behavior that get them off the hook. You will often have a lot of unresolved arguments with a manipulative person, and this is very unhealthy. A key sign of this is that a manipulator will often end an argument or conversation that is not going their way, without you even realizing it. It is important to know how to deal with conflict properly, but the manipulator cannot do that because they are so focused on themselves and always being in the right. Any good relationship will be one in which both people genuinely want to help each other. If you are dealing with someone who can never work through a problem with you, there is a good chance that they are not the right person for you.

8. Manipulative People Prefer To Play On Their Homeground

As we've already established, the personality of a manipulative person is very controlling. A manipulative person will usually insist on meeting or interacting with you in a place where they feel more powerful and in control of the situation. This could be their office, car, home, or any other place where the manipulator feels familiarity and ownership. The manipulator ultimately does this for two reasons. One, they want to retain the upper hand by being in their comfort zone. And two, they want to weaken you by taking you out of yours. This does not have to be just physically, either. A manipulator will try to take you out of your comfort zone emotionally and financially as well. Be cautious of anyone who is never willing to come out of their comfort zone for you or meet you halfway. It is never a good sign.

9. Manipulative People Rationalize Their Behavior

If ever approached about their manipulative words and deeds, a manipulator will make it seem as if it is not a big deal or will shift the blame onto someone else, somehow making you feel bad for them. Usually, though, it is the manipulator who makes a big deal out of things. Until you say something to them about it, and then they fire every cannon they have back at you to distract you from the main topic at hand. Manipulators also have no empathy for the people who have helped them and will even go so far as to attack those people, should they feel defensive or need to cover up one of their actions or deeds. The manipulative person usually knows that they have a problem, but make it out to seem like it is the world who is against them, rather than the other way around. To the manipulative person, nothing they do is ever wrong. Instead, it is always someone else's fault, and there is always an excuse to rationalize why the manipulative person said or did what they did.

10. Manipulative People Shake Your Confidence

Manipulators often go overboard messing around with other people by using low blow jabs and insults. True friends should feel comfortable poking fun at each other harmlessly, but manipulative people always take it a step too far. They do this especially in groups or social situations to undermine others and establish their dominance. If you have a friend that always leaves you feeling less than great about yourself, they could be a manipulator, and you should end your friendship with them immediately.

Manipulative people suck, but if you keep these ten traits of manipulative people in mind when forming new relationships, you should be able to steer clear of the pain and drama of dealing with one.

SIGNS OF MANIPULATION

1. Charm and Niceness

A manipulator may use charm to get power or sex. Charm comes easily to manipulators because they are ruthless and have no qualms about hurting anyone. A reasonably conscientious person might not use the dirty tricks to seduce someone—that a manipulator will eagerly do.

Manipulators are ardent students of human behavior. After spending some time with a person they find out about their needs and desires. Once they find out what you need they provide you with it to get you addicted or dependent on them. If someone is being very charming and alluring to you, think about, what that person could possibly want. Narcissists and psychopaths—the masters of manipulation—are very cruel once you fall in love with them.

2. Denial

Manipulators are experts at lying and denying. If someone hurts you and you bring attention to their bad behavior, but they deny it even though they clearly have behaved badly, then you should be on your guard. Don't let their denial of bad behavior confuse you.

"This 'who....Me?' tactic is a way of playing innocent and invites the victim to feel unjustified in confronting the aggressor about the inappropriateness of their behavior. It's also the way the aggressor gives himself/herself permission to keep right on doing what they want to do."

3. Lying

Lying is a manipulator's most potent weapon. They have an impaired conscience, so they don't feel bad about lying. If there's a chance to get what they want by lying, they most certainly will.

Manipulators usually lie in subtle, covert ways. Manipulators often lie by withholding a significant amount of information from you or by distorting the truth.

Effectively catching a liar can be learned. So to detect early on, whether you are dealing with a manipulator or not, ask them direct questions about his or her employment, family, relatives, friends, place of residence, plans, and so forth. If they give vague, inconsistent or evasive replies to you, this should serve as a red flag.

Every type of con relies upon distracting us from the obvious.

4. Generous With Favors and Gifts

In the beginning of a relationship, a manipulator may be very kind, sympathetic and generous towards you. He may shower you with expensive gifts and favors, which you might interpret as an expression of his love or affection. But actually, he's using them as a form of bribery to get even bigger favors later on.

So when a person showers you with gifts and attention, pay critical attention to the character and intention of that person.

5. Excessive Compliments and Flattery

"Excessive or incongruous compliments should be a signal for you to pay critical attention to what's coming next. Ask yourself, 'What does this person really want of me?' "

6. Forced Teaming

It's a strategy used by manipulators and con artists to create a sense of togetherness with their chosen victim, through the use of the word, "we."

The manipulator tries to project a shared purpose or experience with you, where none exist. He might use phrases such as "we're some team," "how are we going to handle this?" "both of us," "now we've done it," etc.

How do you tell if someone is genuinely trying to be helpful or they are just manipulating you? Listen to your intuition. Do you feel uncomfortable while accepting help? Do you want to refuse but you can't because this will make you appear rude? If yes, then you are dealing with a manipulator.

Women should NOT accept any offer of help that makes them feel uncomfortable.

The best cons make the victim want to participate.

7. Good First Impression

Skilled manipulators often make excellent impressions. They use captivating characteristics like impeccable manners, dazzling looks or a winning smile, etc. to distract people from their real intentions and message. We hardly buy a book after being impressed by its cover, but unfortunately, we take people at face value. With manipulators, you don't get what you see.

A manipulator may give you a very good first impression, but the cracks in their mask will become apparent only after close observation or spending more time with them.

8. Pretending to Be a Victim

A manipulator may pretend as being a victim of circumstances or bad behavior of someone, as a result making you feel sympathy for him or her.

When a person tries to seek your sympathies, carefully observe that person to try to confirm that they are indeed a victim.

So how to tell a false victim from a real one.

A false victim talks about the events that were abusive to them in a calm, cool, and detached way. They appear to get over the emotions of the abusive experience rather quickly, and they don't seem to dwell or obsess over the abusive experiences.

True victims need to reach out for support; it's important for their survival. They seek therapy, God or other saving methods to restore their mental and emotional health. While talking about the abusive experience, they appear confused, jumpy, nervous and afraid. They may cry hysterically—urgency and emotion are in their speech. They do not have the cold, cool demeanor of a lying manipulator. True victims go through the grieving process—shock, denial, and anger to finally the stage of acceptance.

But manipulators pretending to be victims don't try to seek that kind of support. They don't need it because they were not abused. Manipulators pretending to be victims are not seeking kindness and compassion, but they are after a goal, so coolly and in control, they tell you their story.

9. Silent Treatment

Getting "Silent treatment" is an early warning sign that you are dealing with a manipulator. It is a passive aggressive form of emotional abuse in which displeasure, disapproval, and contempt are exhibited through nonverbal gestures while maintaining silence.

Manipulators use silent treatment as a weapon to provoke you into doing something or make you feel less worthy by refusing to acknowledge even your presence. If an act of your behavior is not contributing towards the manipulator's goal, they will use silent treatment as a punishment to communicate their displeasure.

If it is a sadistic manipulator, then they might use silent treatment just to torture you.

Examples of silent treatment might be:

A coworker openly talks to others but refuses to speak to you.

Your roommate is willing to talk to her friends on phone, or bring them in the room and talk to them for hours, but refuses to speak to you.

10. Appearing to Be Selfless

Manipulators keep their intentions, ambitions, desire for power and domination well hidden, so in the first few meetings with a manipulator, you might find him/her to be a selfless and helpful person.

"Covert-aggressives use this tactic to cloak their self-serving agendas in the guise of service to a more noble cause. It's a common tactic but difficult to recognize.By pretending to be working hard on someone else's behalf, covert-aggressives conceal their ambition, desire for power, and a quest for a position of dominance over others."

11. Guilt Tripping

Pay close attention to a person who often tries to make you feel guilty. Chances are, that person is manipulating you.

Manipulators are aware that other people have a different conscience, so they exploit the good nature of their victims to keep them in self-doubting, guilt-ridden, anxious and submissive position.

12. Shaming

If you catch a person often saying insulting remarks or hurtful comments about your weight, family, appearance or employment, etc, then this should be taken as a warning sign—especially of a manipulative friend. Manipulators pay close attention to a person's insecurities and weak points. If you are insecure about your weight or don't like the shape of your nose, they are quick to notice. If you have repeatedly failed an exam, they will make fun of you for it. Our success or physical appearance is not very much in our control so making fun of someone's difficult situation shows the mean and predatory nature of the individual. They often try to pass off their offensive remarks as jokes, but if you pay close attention, your intuition will tell you that the jokes are not funny and have unfriendly overtones. It's their secret attempt to put you down. So, what they gain by doing that?

Manipulators use shaming to make their victim feel inadequate or unworthy, and therefore, become submissive to them. It is a powerful tactic to create a continued sense of personal inadequacy in the victim, thus allowing the manipulator to maintain a position of dominance.

13. Intimidation

Manipulators usually use covert intimidation. Their threats are carefully veiled. If someone makes you feel uncomfortable or you suspect them of manipulation, pay close attention to their non-verbal gestures, expressions, glances, and stares, when they talk to you.

14. Gas Lighting

Perhaps not an early warning sign, but it is a powerful tactic used by manipulators. The term owes its origin to the play Gas Light and its film adaptations, after which it was coined. Since then the term has been used in clinical and research literature. It means twisting reality for a particular purpose.

A manipulator is a genius when it comes to twisting reality to serve their own purposes. It doesn't matter what the truth is, they have a way of ultimately showing you that it really is your own fault and that you aren't seeing things clearly. By the time you accept their version of reality, you have become so mentally sick that you can't trust your own perceptions.

If someone questions your perceptions of reality, do not trust their opinion.
Always listen to your intuition. What it tells you about a person or a situation is right.

15. Rationalization

It is an excuse a manipulative person offers for engaging in hurtful or inappropriate behaviors. It can be an effective tactic especially when the explanation offered makes just enough sense that any reasonably conscientious person is likely to fall for it.

Rationalization serves three primary purposes:

It removes internal resistance the manipulator might have about their harmful action.

It keeps others off their back.

If the manipulator can convince you they are justified in doing what they have been doing, then they are free to pursue their goals.

Manipulators are fine actors. They can pretend to be a victim; they can cry a river whenever they want; they can fake love; they can fake joy or any other emotion. So carefully observe the actions of those who claim to love you, or who try to gain your sympathy by shedding tears.

It's noble to be kind and gentle but select the receivers of your kindness VERY carefully.

16. Diversion

When you are trying to keep a discussion focused on a single issue or behavior (that you consider bad or cruel), but someone changes the subject or dodges the issue, then this should alert you. You might ask yourself, "Why doesn't this person want to discuss it?" "Use distraction and diversion techniques to keep the focus off of their behavior, move us off-track, and keep themselves free to promote their self-serving hidden agendas."

17. Unsettling Stare

Many people believe that eyes are windows to the soul. That eyes do provide some information about the person "particularly when the message they convey to others appears inconsistent with the individual's facial expressions and verbal behavior." In that case, a person should not ignore the information given by eyes.

Some people respond to the emotionless stare of a skilled manipulator with discomfort, while others feel hypnotized by them.

PSYCHOLOGICAL MANIPULATION

The art of manipulation is not about making people do what you want them to do but rather getting them to want to do what you want them to do. The Art of War by Sun Tzu is the perfect book to learn this. As he says in it "we must know thyself and thy enemy".
Psychological manipulation is a type of social influence that aims to change the behavior or perception of others through indirect, deceptive, or underhanded tactics. By advancing the interests of the manipulator, often at another's expense, such methods could be considered exploitative and devious.

First things first: there is a big difference between psychological or emotional manipulation and simple influence. Healthy social influence appears naturally without anyone trying to force it. We may affect others' choices, preferences and judgment without threatening their health and emotional or physical well-being.

In case of psychological manipulation, however, manipulator's goal is to create an imbalance of power in order to exploit others' weaknesses to serve their own interests. The roots of emotional manipulation are quite complex. Generally, the reasons why an individual may choose manipulative behavior include

Personal gain,
Desire for power and superiority,
Desire to control,
Self-esteem issues,
Boredom.

The cycle of manipulation typically includes three stages:
The manipulator discovers a weakness (or emotional hot buttons) of his or her victim;
The manipulator takes advantage of this weakness;
The cycle repeats.
Many victims have one or more of the traits below:

Unhealthy desire to please,
Love addiction (afraid to be single),
Lack of assertiveness,
Fear of confrontation,
Low self-confidence,
Loneliness,
Blurry sense of identity,
Low self-reliance,
External locus of control,
Naivety,
Emotional dependency,
Immaturity.

These character traits often serve as emotional hot buttons that the manipulator uses to his advantage. This doesn't mean that the victim is guilty of abuse. It only means that manipulators prey on this type of people more often. Needless to say, the victims of emotional manipulation are often young or in a situation when they are mentally exhausted and are unable to fight back.

Wondering whether you are being manipulated? Here are some of the most common red flags of psychological manipulation:

Your words are used against you;

The manipulator poses as rescuer but their help leaves you feeling miserable;

The manipulator makes a disturbing statement, and then claims you misunderstood what they said;

You constantly feel guilty;

The manipulator makes you question your own sanity;

If you don't give them what they want, they will withdraw their love and affection;

You are unhappy in this relationship, and yet you fear losing it;

Your relationship feels very complex;

You always feel you are falling short of their expectations;

You feel like you are walking on eggshells;

They are trying to isolate you.

So how do you get people to want to do what you want them to? First you have to learn their true desires and reverse engineer it toward the goal you want to accomplish.

The closer the person is to you, the easier it is to manipulate. The closer the person is to you, the easier it is to manipulate, and yes I said this twice, very important. Thus, romantic partners or mates are the best prospects to test your manipulation skills. And if "manipulation" feels like a bad word, think of it as persuasion.

You want to persuade people. You have to make people feel like it was their choice all along. In general, men want perfectionism and women tend to want wholeness. So what does that mean? Men are usually more easily persuaded by mastery and the ego associated with improvement. So displaying uncertainty on whether or not a man can improve taunts the ego in a gentle way that yields progress. With women, being balanced in many areas in life, especially with relationships of friends and family is a MUST. Thus, suffocating time or impact on specific relationships creates a burning desire to bring it up (balance).

On some level, we all need balance and we all need to sacrifice and focus. But statistically, women tend to lean towards balance while men tend to lean towards focusing on perfectionism.

In the midst of any persuasion tactic, it's wise to never disobey the law or cognitive bias called "liking and loving tendency". What is that? If Adolf Hitler says 2+2=4 and Oprah says 2+2=5, even though we hate Hitler, he is correct and Oprah (loved by many) is wrong. However, most people would believe Oprah because they associate (association bias) her with everything positive. You must care about how you make others feel. Because just like Maya Angelou says, people may forget what you did or said but they will remember the way you made them feel.

Also, most people want to manipulate over the short term. However, the true art of manipulation is really loving the long game. Patience is a virtue. Similarly to how professionals make their "art" looks easy, you have to make the persuasiveness feel and flow effortlessly. It takes time and patience for you to mentally overcome your mental barriers and get your mindset right.

One of the things that mentallyhurt manipulators in this process is not understanding and GOING with Mother Nature. Just like a boulder rolling down the hill, you want to let gravity (nature) pull you. Don't force or go against Mother Nature. When it rains, we adapt by getting an umbrella or jacket. When it is hot, we wear less or light layers of clothing. Basically, I'm saying don't be delusional and adjust to what is. How do you test for delusion? Two ways: doing the right thing in the wrong order is still the wrong thing aka, misprioritization of priorities & having expectations of output from the wrong input. So with people, we have to know their personality type, how they respond to certain environments, and what their personal boundaries are.

So here's the good part. The mental frameworks are out of the way. So how exactly you get them to do the thing? First, you have to lead with the reward. People love the release of the dopamine aka reward. How can the "thing" you want them to do benefit them? Now, don't tell them directly to do it. Studies have shown, 90% of the time, people hate being told what to do. Instead, you help them come to same conclusion on their own "path". People love feeling like it was THEIR idea (not yours). So let them own it. The only real hard part is attaching the "reward" or benefit to the thing. Because if people don't understand how something benefits them, they will likely never do it.

Also, looking at correlations of what people (that do the thing you want to instill) do as well as the "thing". For example, if you want to persuade someone to lose weight and bringingup the word "diet" is hard. Try talking about improved skin complexion (which is indirectly correlated to great diets).

You can lead people to water but sometimes you can't make them drink. So instead, make them THIRSTY. Curiosity wins! Get the person curious about topics and you'll get nature working for you, similar to a boulder rolling down the hill due to gravity. Never disobey all scientific laws, just flow with it.

Best example of manipulation is the scam of higher education. High school students are effortlessly manipulated and curious about the rewards following a worthless degree. K-12, or 13 years of schooling just to ruin ones' credit and take away their "free money", the education system even understands the importance of the "long game".

Social influence is not necessarily negative. For example, people such as friends, family and doctors, can try to persuade to change clearly unhelpful habits and behaviors. Social influence is generally perceived to be harmless when it respects the right of the influenced to accept or reject it, and is not unduly coercive. Depending on the context and motivations, social influence may constitute underhanded manipulation.

Once you have successfully manipulated, never expose yourself because it will disobey liking and loving tendency and people will cut you off. You don't want that. Maintain consciousness of how you are making them feel and try to manipulate, "persuade", for the best, don't be evil.

CPSIA information can be obtained
at www.ICGtesting.com
Printed in the USA
BVHW061027220321
603178BV00004B/486